"Everyone needs to read this book! Bruce Hamsher's passion for God's Word, coupled with an ability to make it real through engaging storytelling, encourages all of us to live out our calling as 'Certified Spiritual Florists.' *Bouquets* is one of the best field guides available for increasing our understanding of how our aroma represents Christ and impacts the lives of those around us."
—*Lisa Troyer, Moody Broadcasting Network*

"With an obvious pastoral perspective, Bruce Hamsher has creatively weaved the bouquets theme throughout his text in a way that will be inspirational to his readers. This theologically sound and relevant resource is a welcome ministry tool for those who are about the task of discipling believers into a deeper relationship with Christ. I intend to recommend it highly to my ministry students."
—*Randy Keeler, Bluffton University*

"Bruce Hamsher invites us to attentiveness in existing friendships and the seemingly routine daily encounters we have in our homes, workplaces, communities, social events, neighborhoods, and churches. *Bouquets* provides a beginning point for us to assess our friendships in the opportunities we have to be God-incarnate. Hamsher calls us to be accountable while encouraging us to deepen our relationships to include faith in Jesus in our conversations. While seeming to state the obvious—many of us can attest to the power of friendships in our conversion and life of Christian discipleship—Hamsher provides fresh awareness of the command of Jesus to be salt and light!"
—*Henry Beun, Central Christian School, Kidron, Ohio*

"*Bouquets* is a beautiful biblical metaphor made contemporary. Daily relationships are the aroma people sense in every encounter. Is the aroma surrounding Christians that of the presence of God? In this delightful book, Bruce Hamsher observes ordinary folk in the Bible (like Onesiphorus, Mephibosheth, or Paul's nephew) and shows how Christians must be the kind of fragrance these exemplified. Here are guides to make serendipitous relationships an intentional expression of divine mercy and love."
—*August H. Konkel, President of Providence College and Seminary*

"Some books on evangelism make you feel guilty. Others are theories and techniques. Not this one. With stories from life and Scripture Bruce Hamsher invites us to embrace the natural adventure of building redemptive relationships and sharing the life-changing Good News along the way. A good devotional inspirational read as well as a good group study text."
—*Marion G. Bontrager, Hesston College*

Bouquets

Bouquets

Intentional Relationships in Making Disciples

Bruce Hamsher

Foreword by Stephen R. Wingfield

Herald Press
Scottdale, Pennsylvania
Waterloo, Ontario

Library of Congress Cataloging-in-Publication Data
Hamsher, Bruce, 1969-
   Bouquets : intentional relationships in making disciples / Bruce
Hamsher.
      p. cm.
   ISBN-13: 978-0-8361-9407-4 (pbk. : alk. paper)
   1. Evangelistic work. 2. Interpersonal relations—Religious
aspects—Christianity. I. Title.
   BV3793.H347 2008
   269'.2—dc22
                                        2007045375

BOUQUETS: INTENTIONAL RELATIONSHIPS IN MAKING
DISCIPLES
Copyright © 2008 by Herald Press, Scottdale, Pa. 15683
   Published simultaneously in Canada by Herald Press,
   Waterloo, Ont. N2L 6H7. All rights reserved
Library of Congress Catalog Card Number: 2007045375
International Standard Book Number: 978-0-8361-9407-4
Printed in the United States of America
Book design by Joshua Byler
Cover by Sans Serif
Study Guide by Matthew Flinner

13 12 11 10 09 08   10 9 8 7 6 5 4 3 2 1

To order or request information please call 1-800-245-7894 or
visit www.heraldpress.com.

To Jocelyn, Micah, Ty, and Cade.

With special thanks to my fellow pastors and to the wonderful churches I've had the pleasure of serving. In many ways, you've helped me write the pages of this book.

Contents

But thanks be to God, who always leads us in triumphal procession in Christ and through us spreads everywhere the fragrance of the knowledge of him. For we are to God the aroma of Christ among those who are being saved and those who are perishing.
—2 Corinthians 2:14-15

Be the aroma!

Foreword

Educators will tell you that, for a student to learn a new skill, he or she must observe that skill being performed. Before a new concept can be adopted and believed it must first be introduced to the student by another person.

The same is true of our Christian witness. Imagine that you feel a call from God to share the Gospel with a tribal group that has never before heard the name of Jesus Christ. If you were to walk into the jungle and immediately begin preaching, chances are they would not immediately accept your words as truth and fall to the ground in repentance. Your words would have to be validated by your commitment to love, acceptance, and forgiveness through your daily life and attitudes as you live among them.

Friendships are essential to success in witnessing and discipleship, and not just casual, fair-weather friendships. We need intentional relationships that go beyond our comfort zones, challenging us to be Jesus with skin on to those who need him. These types of relationships are difficult, causing us to give of ourselves, sometimes beyond what we think our limits are, to give up our free time, resources, our selfish desires. They challenge us to answer that 11 p.m. phone call or knock at the door when we just want to go to bed.

In *Bouquets: Intentional Relationships in Making Disciples*, Bruce Hamsher will challenge your definition and purpose of friendship. He will encourage you to go beyond casual acquaintance in your present relationships in order to demonstrate Jesus' love through Christ-like character. Bruce's insightful illustrations from Scripture pinpoint examples of how individuals from the Old and New testaments viewed relationships and used their influence to draw others to God.

The premise for Bruce's book is that our relationships are crucial to our witness. The way we live out our Christian faith may make or break a non-believer's opinion of God. We all know people who have been turned off to Christianity because of a bad experience within the church. Those we are in relationship with see us every day. They observe our responses to them and our circumstances. Whether we are consciously aware of it or not, we are representing Jesus, either positively or negatively, every moment of every day. That is how others are going to view God—by the way we live our lives in front of them.

Are we showing Christ through our relationships? Do we demonstrate his unconditional love for us by the way we relate to others? Jesus is the example we must follow. We see him mingling with sinners—those with messy, unethical, immoral lives. But he didn't just pat them on the back when he happened to pass them on the street. When they came to him for help, healing, or comfort, he didn't just spout trite phrases like, "Chin up!" or "When the going gets tough, the tough get going!" No. He *intentionally* sought them out time and time again. Remember Zacchaeus? Jesus told him, "Come down *immediately*. I *must* stay at your house today" (Luke 19:5, emphasis added). Notice the urgency is Jesus' words. This is no reluctant request to have dinner with a sinner. This is a burning desire to spend quality time with someone loved by God.

There are times when Jesus was emotionally and physically weary, but through the Holy Spirit he still found strength to minister. In Matthew 14:13-14, we find Jesus in one of the darkest days of his life. He has just received news that his friend, John the Baptist, has been beheaded. Scripture says, "When Jesus heard what had happened, he withdrew by boat privately to a solitary place. Hearing of this, the crowds followed him on foot from the towns. When Jesus landed and saw a large crowd, he had compassion on them and healed their sick."

Imagine that! Jesus just wants to be alone to grieve the death of a dear friend. But the people won't leave him alone long enough to do that! He could have chosen to walk away; he had a legitimate reason for needing time to himself. But even in his sadness, Jesus set aside his desires, and even his needs, to love others. Most people would say that's going above and beyond the call of duty. But as Bruce will share, God calls us to higher levels of service, perhaps asking us to minister when we don't think we have anything to give.

The truth Bruce shares out of his own life experience exemplifies what he teaches in this book. In his own candid style, he allows us glimpses into his past, to learn by his example and, in some cases, through his mistakes.

The study guide provided at the end of the book will help apply the principles outlined in each chapter. The thought-provoking questions and Scripture readings offer a foundation for reflection and allow God to encourage you and perhaps put his finger on areas of your own relationships that need his touch.

In a practical, sound, and biblically-based manner, Bruce has captured the essence of what it means to "be the aroma" of God to those around us. Bruce offers clear, concise guidance on developing purposeful relationships. As you learn the importance of being honest, real, and available in your relationships, you will be overwhelmed by the flow of blessing that will result. Your friendships will never be the same.

Stephen R. Wingfield
Steve Wingfield Evangelistic Association

Introduction

An elderly farmer was known in his small community as the town grump. He was incessantly negative, nasty, and noncompliant to most everyone he met. For years, area pastors were encouraged to visit and talk with him. One by one they went, but they were unable to change him. Imagine then, the surprise when word got out that this ninety-year-old farmer had prayed the sinner's prayer, asked Jesus into his heart, and was now a changed man.

How did the gospel finally penetrate his heart? Part of the answer had to do with the farmer's seed salesman of the past forty years, who for several decades had patiently and methodically cultivated an intentional relationship with the farmer. The cultivating yielded an eternal crop.

For me, the story raises a question: With whom is God more pleased: this seed salesman or Billy Graham? It's clear that God is equally pleased with both of them.

As a believer, you are the seed salesperson. You've been given a territory that is uniquely yours to "do good works, which God prepared in advance for [you] to do" (Ephesians 2:10). As you travel the streets and roads of your assigned area, your initial job is to simply plant the seed. Scripture says that as you're faithful in planting the seed, others then come along to water it. Ultimately God himself will make it grow (see 1 Corinthians 3:6).

This book is an invitation to discover the power of intentional relationships in our everyday lives. We'll observe what happens when people reach out to others in their specific circles of influence, all in the name of Christ. I intend to encourage and motivate you as you live out Jesus' call to "go and make disciples" (Matthew 28:19). Whether you are age eight or eighty, you can do this! May God eternally bless your efforts as you faithfully live out this call.

1

Bouquets to the Living

Being God's Fragrance to Others

Key Points

- *Wouldn't it make more sense to give of ourselves now?*
- *How about sending bouquets to the living?*
- *We cannot live our lives being "wish-I-wouldas." We need to belong to the "glad-I-didda" tribe.*

Occasionally I drive through a neighboring town that has a large bakery on one of its busier streets. If it's early morning, I sometimes slow the car, roll down the window, and savor the wonderful fragrance wafting from the bakery. For a few moments, everything seems right with the world.

Consider things such as warm, freshly baked bread, fresh-cut flowers, your husband's cologne, your wife's perfume, freshly brewed coffee, or chocolate-chip cookies right out of the oven. We'd all agree that smelling something pleasant often refreshes us, wakes us up, makes us smile. Such aromas may be the reason you even now have a desire to go bake, or at least eat, some of those cookies. Perhaps you will do so later today or tomorrow.

So, what do these scrumptious smells, awesome aromas, and fantastic fragrances have to do with your Christian life? They actually have everything to do with your faith walk because they are descriptive of who you are to be to the world around you. Spiritually, it is how you are to be with your family, your spouse, your co-workers, your neighbors, grumpy people, happy people—everyone you meet. As you go about your days, you are called to spread everywhere "the fragrance of the knowledge" of Christ (2 Corinthians 2:14).

In other words, because God loves you so much, he sent Christ to show you the way through the challenges of this life and to lead you in a royal, triumphant procession toward the winner's circle, where you'll receive your eternal crown. Because as a believer you're assured that Jesus did indeed pay it all, you can now choose to live with this wonderful fragrance coming forth and oozing from within you.

Scripture is packed full with these exhortations:

> Praise be to . . . the God of all comfort, who comforts us in all our troubles, so that we can comfort those in any trouble with the comfort we ourselves have received from God. (2 Corinthians 1:3-4)

> Let us not become weary in doing good. . . . As we have opportunity, let us do good to all people, especially to those who belong to the family of believers. (Galatians 6:9-10)

> If anyone speaks, he should do it as one speaking the very words of God. (1 Peter 4:11)

In our culture, we frequently wait until someone has died

before we send the most beautiful bouquet of flowers we've ever sent to that person. It's certainly a nice gesture for the family, but it does absolutely nothing for the deceased. Wouldn't it make much more sense if we would give of ourselves and share this fragrance while we're still living? How about sending some bouquets to the living?

I told someone recently to save the money at my funeral. I'd much rather receive a fresh bouquet now, today, while I can enjoy it, appreciate it, and say thank you for it. And who knows, I may even pass one of my own on to someone else. The apostle Paul wrote, "For we are to God the aroma of Christ" (2 Corinthians 2:15). Because you are part of the body of Christ, then, his aroma should naturally come forth from within you.

Most homes have a unique scent. Remember Grandma's house and its distinctive smell? In a spiritual sense too, your very name and life have distinct aromas attached to them. If I were a silent, invisible listener in your home or workplace, what would I notice? What would I say you smell like? Is it the aroma of Christ?

Many of us are fanatics about planning. We often plan things down to each half hour of the day. This may be beneficial, but it's imperative to remain flexible enough to allow "God-appointments" to interrupt our tight schedules. I know of a pastor who works very hard at being what he calls "unbusy" so that he can be available when these unforeseen God-appointments arise. I suggest you consider doing the same. This is a counter-cultural idea, but so is the entire gospel. But because you literally have no idea what will happen tomorrow, make the most of every opportunity each day, starting today.

Read closely these words from a wise man named Solomon:

> Give portions to seven, yes to eight, for you do not
> know what disaster may come upon the land. If clouds
> are full of water, they pour rain upon the earth. Whether
> a tree falls to the south or to the north, in the place

where it falls, there will it lie. Whoever watches the wind will not plant; whoever looks at the clouds will not reap. (Ecclesiastes 11:2-4)

Scripture calls us here and in many other places to be intentional about giving our time, resources, and energy—today, while we can. If you think you can give seven, think it over. It may be possible to give eight. You must be as generous as you can while you have the opportunity to do so. We cannot live our lives being "wish-I-wouldas." We need to belong to the "glad-I-didda" tribe.

You just don't know what will happen and when it will happen. If the clouds are full of water, it is going to rain, and you can't do anything about it. The next time a big storm blows its way through your town, go out and try to direct the raindrops and bring order to the wind patterns. Good luck!

A large tree may naturally become weak and begin to fall down. Imagine the futility of seeing this tree begin its descent toward your house with you standing beneath it, yelling and shouting at it, attempting to redirect its landing spot by telling it precisely where it should come to rest. Sorry, but it will lie wherever it wants to, and you can't do anything about it. Isn't this so indicative of life?

If you wait around for perfect weather, the seeds will never be planted. If you wait for the perfect situation to give your bouquet of blessings, you'll probably never do it. As Christians, we are not called to make excuses. Because Christ has not left us in the dark, our job then is to be a shining light into someone else's darkness, all for the glory of God.

As a Christian, you are a sweet fragrance to God. The best picture here is that of a flower. A flower gives off a sweet fragrance to our sense of smell, and therefore it is acceptable to us. In the same way, as you go about your days and as your lifestyle spreads this fragrance of Christ, your aroma is not only more acceptable to others, but ultimately is then fully acceptable and received by God himself as your offering to him.

I encourage you to think about these things the next time you attend a viewing or funeral. Better yet, learn to be a giver of these bouquets before you arrive at the next one. Consider why we only give bouquets to the deceased. Why not reorient our thinking and consistently give bouquets to the living?

In your newly found profession as a certified spiritual florist, who then will receive your fresh-smelling bouquet today or tomorrow?

2

Rock Droppers

Jesus and a Sinner

Key Points

- *Are you primarily a rock thrower or a rock dropper?*
- *When someone sins, instead of talking about them, why not do something for them?*
- *Mercy is compassion in action.*

In the eighth chapter of John's Gospel, we meet a woman who was caught in the act of adultery. If we heard her recall her personal encounter with Jesus, it might sound something like this. Listen for your own life story in her words.[*]

> I will never forget that day they burst into the room and dragged me from his arms. What shame and humiliation! I could not even cover my nakedness. They pulled

[*] Partially adapted from Liz Curtis Higgs, *Really Bad Girls of the Bible* (Colorado Springs: WaterBrook Press, 2000).

me out through the doorway and into the courtyard. As I tried to hide my face, they forced me to stand in front of another condemning group of men just like themselves. I wept, my tears burning my cheeks. Their harsh words rolled so effortlessly off their lips—ugly, demeaning, and cruel names.

As the circle of men opened up, there stood another man. I stole a glance at him but turned my eyes away, unwilling to bear more condemnation. Someone spoke to this man, calling him teacher.

"Teacher," he said, "this woman was caught in the act of adultery. In the law, Moses commanded us to stone such women. Now then, what do you say?"

I cringed as I heard my punishment spoken aloud. I was guilty. I had broken the law. With this realization, any trace of hope disappeared. This life I was living had now brought me to my death.

I stood there, waiting for this man to speak. Only silence.

Again I quickly looked up, fearing the teacher's response. But he wasn't standing over me with condemning eyes. He was kneeling, writing something on the ground with his finger. I didn't know why he was kneeling or what he was writing. All I knew was that it seemed he was the only one not enjoying this trial. He didn't stare at my half-naked body. He was treating me as a person, a person of worth.

As he continued writing, the group of men shouted at him, plaguing him with questions about my punishment. He then slowly stood up, and I watched as he looked each one in the eye and said, "If any one of you is without sin, let him be the first to throw a stone at her." Then he bent down and continued writing.

I leaned over, stiffening, expecting the blows. As I

waited for my death to begin, I heard thuds. The men were dropping their rocks in the dirt and walking away.

One solitary sentence by this man had turned them all from rock throwers to rock droppers. Tears of disbelief began to fall as I looked to the man called teacher. He stood again and walked toward me.

With just one glance, his eyes revealed what seemed to be limitless love and acceptance. "Where did the rock droppers go?" he asked. "Has no one condemned you?" Still filled with awe, I replied, "No one, sir." Then came freedom, as he said, "Then neither do I condemn you. Go now and leave your life of sin."

I was guilty. I knew it and he knew it. The law pointed me to death, but when the teacher spoke, the law had no choice but to relent. I was free, and I did nothing to deserve it. It was simply a spoken word by the teacher, declaring my pardon, that gave me life. Not only life, but new life—a new beginning, a new identity, a new freedom.

What about you? As you go through life and encounter people in many different situations, are you primarily a rock thrower or a rock dropper? What is it about us that revels in pointing out others' sins while clearly choosing to overlook our own? Why is it that if I'm not committing the same sin you are, the dam of my judgment lets loose?

It is clear to me that, as a sinner, I've just heard my life's story as told by this adulterous women. If I were to be a rock thrower, my target would be the center of my own back. Why would anyone willingly throw rocks at himself and bring about his own death?

It's fascinating to see how the places in Scripture where Jesus gives life are often the same places where we give judgment. How about trying this? When someone sins, don't talk *about* them; do something *for* them. It's what Jesus did for you and me and for all humanity!

As Christ shows us in this story, our acceptance of sinners doesn't mean we approve of the sinful behavior. It simply means we approve of and are in favor of that person also receiving the mercy we've received hundreds of times.

This reality of not getting what I deserve was never so real to me as when I found myself standing before a judge in a real court of law somewhere in my teen years. It had seemed appropriate to my friends and I to go out and demolish twenty-four mailboxes and have a blast doing it. It was fun, and we had the neighborhood bragging rights—until a dreaded phone call a few days later informing me that we "got caught."

After recovering from that horrible feeling of my heart sinking into my stomach and just sort of sitting there for several weeks, it was time to face the music. As I stood there and faced the judge, I fully realized that I was completely at his mercy. He had done his homework and knew a good bit about me. He knew what my grades were, who my friends were, and what my reputation was. He asked me if I had been drinking and why in the world I would do such a thing. I answered no and said, "It just kind of happened."

After bracing myself for a lecture and the sentence, something magically and mercifully happened. He went on to share a story from his own youthful years about the time when he was walking out of a roller-skating rink and bashed out someone's car lights with his skates. He said he wasn't sure why he did it, but figured that it "just kind of happened." He had determined that I wasn't likely to be a lifelong criminal and gave me a reduced sentence that consisted primarily of going back to those I had wronged, paying for new mailboxes and agreeing that I would "sin no more."

Mercy is good, and the mercy flowed that day.

How do we define mercy? A good place to start might be to first point out what mercy is not. Mercy isn't pretending to care or to be compassionate. It's not becoming self-righteous like the Pharisees, who thought they were getting brownie points from

God by giving to the poor. Mercy isn't bothering to show kindness only when you think there's something in it for you. Nor is it merely having pity on others.

So then, what is true mercy? According to Scriptures that describe our Lord's mercy, I believe we can sum it up by declaring that mercy is *compassion that goes into action*. It is doing something with the feelings you have for someone.

The Bible proposes some questions: "Suppose a brother or sister is without clothes and daily food. If one of you says to him, 'Go, I wish you well; keep warm and well fed,' but does nothing about his physical needs, what good is it?" (James 2:15-16). "If anyone has material possessions and sees his brother in need but has no pity on him, how can the love of God be in him?" (1 John 3:17).

Suppose someone you know is living without the spiritual armor of God and without a trace of spiritual food. Will you continue to be content by feeling sorry for them? Or will you spiritually show true mercy and do something about it?

True mercy is putting that compassion into action. Jesus is the greatest example of this kind of mercy. In his encounter with the adulterous woman, he not only physically saved her life, he also gave her the opportunity to embrace a new spiritual life she had seemingly never known. Also, in the story of the woman at the well in chapter 4 of John's Gospel, we see how his power and presence transformed the woman from a five-time divorcee to an anointed evangelist who reached her community with the gospel message.

Christ clearly majored in misfits and outcasts. He healed the sick, made the lame walk, loved the lepers, gave sight to the blind, made deaf ears hear, gave life to the dead . . . We could go on and on, but the point is that he saw those in need, and he showed them compassion by intentionally choosing to do something about it. A truly awesome thing about Jesus' mercy is that it meets us both physically and, better yet, spiritually. He loves and forgives everyone, from loose-living prostitutes to dishonest tax collectors to regular old sinners like us.

There's a story about a prize-winning horse that had a disease in its hoof. Because of the severity, the horse's owners knew it would have to be "put down." But shortly before this happened, a new invention had been developed: a steel hoof prosthesis that could be drilled into the bone of the horse's leg. This news changed everything. The prosthesis saved the horse's life—from no hope to a living hope.

This is precisely what mercy does for you and me. Peter shouts it out when he says, "Praise be to the God and Father of our Lord Jesus Christ! In his great mercy he has given us new birth into a living hope through the resurrection of Jesus Christ from the dead, and into an inheritance that can never perish, spoil or fade—kept in heaven for you" (1 Peter 1:3-4).

Because of his mercy, death has no hold on you as a believer. Your future is one of eternal life.

Here's where the rubber hits the road: Where do you see needs in your community today? Where can you willingly choose to put your compassion into action? What real-life situations and circumstances are available to you? And who do you know that is spiritually piled full of guilt? Who could really use, instead of more judgment, some genuine mercy? Most importantly, what will you do about it?

May all of us see the uselessness of having only sorrow for or mere pity on someone else. God Almighty, in his mercy, has provided a way for you to be with him forever. He saw your great need to be saved from evil and knew you were incapable of saving yourself. In seeing your desperate need, he put his compassion into action by sending his Son to die a death only he could die and to become the sacrificial lamb that would pay the heavy price of sin in the place of you and me. Our sins can now be forgiven and, by his mercy, we can fully embrace the reality of our eternal heavenly home.

Won't you intentionally extend this kind of mercy very soon, with the hope and prayer that it will touch someone for eternity?

3

Squeezing Your Sponge

Onesiphorus Searches for Paul

Key Points

• *Onesiphorus seemed more concerned about Paul's well-being than his own needs or personal reputation.*
• *He had decided to put forth a great deal of effort in reaching Paul, seeking him out in intentional, diligent ways for the specific purpose of ministering to him.*

Two neighboring rival schools challenged each other to a race. The two best runners for each team often ran together in the off-season and thus became very good friends. As this much-anticipated race began and progressed, the two were running stride-for-stride. As they rounded the last turn, one began to take a short lead. The one who was slightly behind tried desperately to catch up, and somehow their feet got tangled together, causing the second-place runner to fall hard onto the track, yelling and grabbing his bloody ankle. When his friend, who was only twenty-five yards from the finish line realized what had happened, he stopped running, went back to help, and lost the race.

What do you think the spectators who witnessed this race remember about it? How many persons five years later could even recall who eventually won the race?

Consider the story of Jackie Robinson. Jackie was the first African-American to play baseball in the major leagues. Breaking baseball's color barrier, he faced hostile crowds in every stadium. While playing one day in his home stadium of Ebbets Field in Brooklyn, he committed a crucial error. As he stood there at second base, already feeling awful, the crowd began to boo loudly. Without saying a word, shortstop Pee Wee Reese went over to Jackie, put his arm around him, and faced the crowd. Suddenly the fans grew quiet. Robinson later recalled how that arm around his shoulder saved his career.

We see this kind of dedicated devotion given freely to the apostle Paul during the last days of his life while he was bound in a Roman prison. In a dungeon-like cell unfit even for animals, the core elements of his faith had not wavered. Yet understandably he needed someone with skin on to be with him. Paul lists several men who had deserted him in his condition while he points out one man who had not.

This unidentified man was someone named Onesiphorus. How do we know? In 2 Timothy, Paul writes, "May the Lord show mercy to the household of Onesiphorus, because he often refreshed me and was not ashamed of my chains. On the contrary, when he was in Rome, he searched hard for me until he found me" (1:16-17). Onesiphorus was singled out as the one person who continued to refresh Paul, regardless of his situation or location.

Refresh means to renew well-being and vigor, to cheer up and revive. I still remember my favorite water fountain in the entire high school building and the way the water flowed from it after basketball practice. I had to run down several steps and through a back hallway to get to it, but once I arrived and experienced the perfect flow combined with the perfect temperature of the water, I could just drink and drink and drink. It was pure refreshment. This is the kind of intentional, spiritual refreshment Onesiphorus brought to Paul's very soul.

In looking at these verses, we see a game plan mapped out for all of us as we go about giving our bouquets to the living. We see foremost that Onesiphorus must have had a true concern, because Paul talks about his refreshing services as occurring not once or twice, but often. It's common for us to say to someone in need, "Now, if there's anything I can do, just call." This is often said with good intentions, but typically the person in need doesn't call, then we get busy and, well, you know the rest. Truth is, if you're really concerned, it will produce a call to action. Your follow-through will show whether your concern is real or make-believe.

Second, it's apparent that he also had true compassion that produced within him courage to step out. There was a reason these other men had deserted Paul and had stopped coming to see him. He was not well liked, and Onesiphorus took on himself a substantial risk to his own well-being. In short, it was hard, dirty work to minister to Paul in the condition he was in. But Onesiphorus seemed much more concerned about Paul's well-being than his own needs or reputation. He literally risked being ridiculed, mocked, and even punished unjustly. But thankfully his compassion for Paul won out.

Third, Onesiphorus displayed a solid, true commitment as "he searched hard . . . until he found" Paul. It was this tenacious commitment that produced a true completion of what was started. He had decided to put forth a great deal of effort in reaching Paul, seeking him out in intentional, diligent ways for the specific purpose of ministering to him.

The impressive thing about his effort is that he was seemingly under no obligation to visit and minister to Paul. He wasn't Paul's pastor, and he wasn't on the visitation committee from church. He simply made it a top priority and followed through. In doing so, he literally had to search through a maze of damp, dingy, and smelly prison cells to find him. But he made no excuses. He simply persevered until he found Paul.

Onesiphorus's example reminds me of the joke about the man who was running errands in his hometown late one Saturday evening. While sitting in his car at a traffic light, he glanced over to a nearby parking lot and saw a man he knew being robbed and beaten up. When he saw this man later, he told him, "I was just about to get out and help you, but just then the light turned green." Isn't this indicative of how we often are when it comes to meeting the needs of others around us?

I'm reminded of a piece of property I see on a certain drive through the countryside. On it is an almost-built house with a driveway grown over with grass. It's clear that the builders had started out with great intentions, but for some reason they stopped working. If we're honest, this is what happens to many of our outreach efforts. We have great intentions and start things out with a great deal of energy and ambition, only to allow some lame excuse to douse the fire. Paul tells the church at Corinth that they are to "finish the work, so that your eager willingness to do it may be matched by your completion of it" (2 Corinthians 8:11).

Who do you know that is sitting in an emotional, physical, or spiritual dungeon? Who could use some good old-fashioned refreshment? Will your eagerness to meet a need be matched by completion, by you actually doing something about it?

I invite you to see your life as a sponge and to imagine three buckets beside you. The first bucket is full of water and represents the living water of Christ. The second is one-quarter full of water, and the third is empty. As the sponge, you fully immerse yourself in the first bucket, the living water, and let it fill up every available space. Once full, you then squeeze and empty yourself into the second bucket, which obviously needs more water to become full. You repeat this process several times until the second bucket is full and now prepared to share its water.

You then immerse yourself in the second bucket, and pour the water into bucket number three, which has an even greater need than the second bucket did. As this is repeated several times, bucket number three slowly becomes filled as well.

But how can it be that all three buckets are now full? Little wonder that Jesus himself says, "Whoever drinks the water I give him will never thirst. Indeed, the water I give will become in him a spring of water welling up to eternal life" (John 4:14). Because Christ provides an eternal spring, the first bucket will never run out of the water. You can immerse yourself in it again and again. Then buckets number two and three and four and five can be filled as well.

As you consider such things as water, sponges, buckets, a weird name like Onesiphorus, hard work, and needy situations, and as you contemplate being intentional about diligently meeting the needs of others around you starting today, consider who will be your Paul.

4

The Extra Mile

Making Time While You Have It

Key Points

• *It's crucial that, starting today, we lighten our schedules.*
• *Being intentional means reaching out and giving of ourselves, especially to those who cannot pay us back.*

Three apprentice devils were coming to earth to carry out their first assignment. As they met with Satan, he asked them what strategy they planned to follow. The first one said he would simply convince persons that there is no God. Satan told him how that approach wouldn't work because almost all people know in their heart of hearts that there is a God. The evidence is just too great.

The second one quickly chimed in and said he would tell people that there is no hell. Again Satan stated that wouldn't work because, in his words, "There is so much evil on earth, they must know there is a hell."

The third one thought for a moment and then exclaimed, "I'll tell them that there is no hurry."

"Go," said Satan with a mighty laugh, "tell them that, and you will ruin them by the thousands."

*The apostle Paul was a great missionary who spent the latter part of his life bringing the good news of Jesus Christ to anyone who would listen. Beatings, shipwrecks, and imprisonment were all a part of his storied résumé, all because he wanted persons to know this Jesus who had so radically changed his life.

By about the year AD 65, Paul was in the last months of his life. He was a prisoner, awaiting trial in Rome, and only Luke was by his side. A thousand miles from home, Paul wrote a last letter to his young friend and fellow minister, Timothy. Paul appeals to Timothy to come quickly because time is growing short. "Do your best to come to me quickly," he writes, then urges, "Do your best to get here before winter" (2 Timothy 4:9, 21).

A question we might ask here is, why before winter? Paul makes this specific request for a good reason. It was not only because the time was growing short for him, but primarily because of the approaching bad weather and the danger of traveling by sea during the winter months. Sea captains of the first century would not sail after a certain date, and Paul knew that if Timothy waited too long, he wouldn't be able to come until spring.

In an ideal world, we'd like to think that Timothy didn't waste a single day. We imagine him reading this letter and immediately setting sail for Rome. We envision him hurrying to Paul, sitting with him in his cell, listening and learning all he could of his mentor's undeniable faith in Jesus Christ. Finally then, he would be right by his side as Paul gave his life as his final offering and witness. We would like to think that Timothy was there. But if he were to make it, it would have to be before winter or never. It is rather vague as to what Timothy actually did.

---

* This narrative is partly adapted from a 1915 sermon called "Come Before Winter" by Clarence MacCartney.

Let's wonder for a moment what would happen if Timothy did what we often do. Suppose he says to himself, "Paul obviously needs me, and I must get to Rome right away. But first, there are some things I need to take care of here at home." Arriving then about a week later, Timothy inquires about the next ship to Rome and is told that the last one of the season left just yesterday. With this news, one can almost hear the groan and feel his agony. There's nothing to do now but wait. He had his chance, but missed it by one day. All through the long winter, he's anxiously left wondering what is happening to his dear friend in Rome.

In the spring, he sails on the first ship out of the port and rushes to the prison, only to find Paul's cell empty. He then diligently searches the city until he hears the words that fill him with shame: "Timothy, you're here at last. Paul was expecting you. However, he died this past winter. Timothy, every time the jailer put his key in the lock, Paul hoped it was you. He left you this message: 'Give Timothy my love when he arrives, my dear son in the faith.'"

If that was the way it turned out, as it so often does, Timothy's anguish would be unbearable. He'd be crushed to realize that he had failed to go the extra mile and arrive before winter.

There are things that will never be done unless they are done right now. There are opportunities that appear only once and then are gone, and there is no way of getting them back again. There are persons in your life who won't be around next year at this time. The winter will pass and spring will come with its promise of new life. But some of your best opportunities and some of your dearest friends may be gone.

Each day of life, there are voices calling to us, "Please, over here! Come now; I need you today. Tomorrow will be too late." These voices are often hard to hear; they get lost in the noise of our everyday lives. Sadly, there have also been times when we have chosen not to hear them because our self-centered nature fears what they will ask of us. We have an intense fear of commitment.

But these voices are important, and what we do in response to them shows who we really are at the core.

Be honest. How often do you send bouquets to the dead rather than the living?

Here are some positive things you can do for that longing voice calling, "Do your best to come to me soon."

- Make time for someone *after* they no longer need you.
- Share freely with others some of your deepest, heartfelt feelings. These are among the most precious gifts that *you alone* can offer.
- Make yourself available to someone who may be waiting to hear from you, someone who needs your love and attention.
- Share your time by offering your words, a visit, a phone call, or an email.
- Through your presence, offer the gift of your prayers and support to lift a heavy heart with a pressing burden.

It's crucial that we *choose* to lighten our schedules. When we shut off the noise of ourselves and clear our minds, we can actually hear, listen, and be open to the Lord's instructions. We are told many times to be there for one another, to feed the hungry, to clothe the naked, and to do these things in both physical and spiritual ways. We know this, and yet many of us lay his instructions aside until tomorrow.

You feel that nudge, but you bargain and say, "Tomorrow, tomorrow." You mean to offer a word of encouragement, but never get around to it. You want to write a letter or make a call, but it never gets done. You desire to share Christ with a co-worker. You intend to get serious about your Christian faith. You hope to read the Bible and pray more.

But do we really want to pray and read the Bible? In short, we all have great intentions, but time, laziness, and the trivial things of life sap our strength and divert our attention until the day comes when the desire is gone and the seeds of complacency and mediocrity take root.

Jesus specifically tells his disciples, "A new command I give you: Love one another. As I have loved you, so you must love one another. By this all men will know that you are my disciples, if you love one another" (John 13:34-35). With this command, Jesus is not talking here of a human, neighborly type of love or of the love with which I simply treat you the same way that I want to be treated. Jesus' new command speaks of his deeper, spiritual love that lives within the believer. It means that I love you not because I feel obligated, or I probably should, or because I know you'll love me back. It means that I intentionally reach out and give of myself, especially to those who cannot pay me back. This new command of selfless, sacrificial love is important because it's precisely the kind of love Jesus shows us. It's the real mark of a true disciple because it shows the spiritual love of Christ to a hurting and needy world.

Today's opportunities may never be repeated. Consider how the sleeping disciples in the garden never had another chance to pray with Jesus in his darkest hour of despair. *Now* is the time to share the love of Christ with someone else. Who is that one person you will minister to?

What would happen if every person reading this would minister in an intentional way to just one other person. It could change entire churches and communities! Don't put it off any longer. Now is the time to lace up your shoes and walk the extra mile.

.

5

Predictably Unpredictable

Saving Uncle Paul

Key Points

- *We can never place God in a predictable box.*
- *God will use any method and any person necessary to carry out his will.*
- *This thing we know: God is never limited in whatever he does or allows.*

The Sunday morning service had been flowing smoothly. The pastor was in the same place he always was prior to preaching, standing by a behind-the-pulpit pew. It was a tradition in his church that everyone would stand and sing a hymn right before the sermon. So there he was, singing away. Near the end of the song however, out of the corner of his eye, something caught his attention. A young couple was standing in the second row of pews and softly talking and giggling with each other. It seems that this young man's zipper was down and his newlywed wife had just informed him of this embarrassing situation. As the pastor glanced down at the minor commotion, he saw the young man looking over to his wife, smiling and whispering something in her ear.

At the same time, he was pulling up his zipper. Here's where the fun begins.

It was also tradition that a group of elderly women would sit on the front pew and remain seated during this time of singing. Well, as the young husband was looking over at his wife and zipping up his pants, his zipper also took with it a few strands of the hair of the woman sitting right in front of him. As the song leader invited everyone to "please be seated," the young man sat down, and off came the elderly woman's wig.

How would you like to compose yourself and begin preaching after witnessing that? I wouldn't have believed this story was true if the pastor hadn't told it to me first-hand.

We've all learned that, indeed, life is full of surprises. Just when we think we've got it all figured out, something new surprises us. The same is true with God's work in each of our lives. Many of us have learned that just when we think we have God figured out, something happens that blows us away. We'd do well to remember that God's thoughts are above our thoughts and his ways above our ways (see Isaiah 55:8-9). We can never place God in a box.

In Scripture, God has pulled many surprises. The apostle Paul went from being a persecutor and a murderer of Christians to a writer of at least a dozen books of the Bible. Peter went from promising to never deny Christ, to repeatedly doing so, to then becoming the rock on which the church was built. David went from the murder-conspiracy boardroom, to the satisfying of his flesh, to becoming best known as a man after God's own heart. The motley bunch of men known as the disciples were blue-collar nobodies without proper education or credentials. They were slow to grasp what Jesus was teaching. At one point,

Jesus wondered how they could be so dull and dense in their lack of understanding his parables. Yet God took this pitiful bunch and equipped them to carry out the gospel message. It's because of them that we know it today.

In Acts 23, we see again how God pulled a surprise in a rather obscure story involving an unlikely hero. Paul had just appeared before the Sanhedrin, the ruling body of the Jews. The Jews were hoping to convince the Romans that Paul was worthy of death. Divinely, the court had been thrown into disarray with the conservative Pharisees arguing against the liberal Sadducees. They had Paul in their grasp and had the chance to get rid of him, but they blew it. The Romans took Paul back into custody in a holding cell.

Later, the Jews realized their mistake. But they didn't give up; they plotted to kill Paul. They would convince the chief priests and elders to summon Paul again into the court's presence so they could further question him. Then, when he was on his way to the court, they would attack him and end his life. They were so serious about this that more than forty men took a vow not to eat or drink until Paul was dead.

Then Paul's unnamed nephew comes on the scene and to the rescue. Paul's sister's son heard about the plot and didn't ignore it or let it pass. To him, this wasn't just anybody; it was Uncle Paul. He was young but yet old enough to realize the seriousness of this threat and the danger Paul was facing. He obviously cared for his uncle and went to him right away.

Take note of where he had to go. He went by himself into the barracks, around all kinds of soldiers and guards. This must have been quite intimidating, frightening, and difficult for him, especially at his age. Yet we see him displaying great courage and audacity. He knew what needed to be done and was intentional about doing it. If this young man had not gone to Paul with this news, we have every reason to believe that Paul would've been seized and killed. Paul was totally helpless on his own, and by intervening for Paul, his nephew was a symbol of Christ. This young man's desire was to be a catalyst in saving Paul's life.

Like Paul's nephew, are you caring and courageous enough to respond to the needs around you and to carry out any task for the Lord, even if it means going "into the barracks"?

Though we do not know what the future holds, we do know who holds the future. We must be ready to willingly respond with boldness to the surprises we encounter. For some, it may be a surprise that you're even reading this book and that you feel a strange tug and compassion to live it out. If you're like me, your own salvation may have been a surprise when you received it, as you considered and continue to be reminded at times of what you were in your sin and where you are now in his grace.

Where we've been and where we are now may be a surprise to us, but it is not to God. Your circumstances may surprise you tomorrow morning, but they do nothing to the promise of hope and your future as a believer in Jesus Christ. This coming week you may be the recipient of a surprise or, better yet, you may become like Paul's nephew: you may very well be chosen by your Creator to be the surprise factor for someone else in their difficult dilemma.

This much we know: God is never limited in anything he does or allows. He is equally present through both our joys and our sorrows, our praises and our trials. Consider this story of a friend of mine. He had made many bad choices and was living a lifestyle doomed to failure. He was dealing and taking drugs while living in the party scene. You name it, he had experienced it. But a surprise was waiting for him when he got a job with a Christian employer.

Over time, he and his boss became friends, and the boss helped lead him to the Lord. His life soon became a vibrant, beaming testimony of God's grace and love. As he continued to grow in his faith, he influenced many other people and was a true blessing to be around. He got married, and he and his wife were expecting a child when tragedy struck. He was in a car crash and died at the hospital.

Here, more surprises happened. Several of his younger brothers, who had followed in their older brother's sinful footsteps, attended the funeral and were obviously gripped by the reality of what had happened. One by one, they eventually each made a personal commitment to Christ. They've since mentioned that it took the death of their brother to make them see the light. It took his dying to make them live, which shows us that God is never limited in anything he does or allows.

In the spiritual realm of things, Satan is known for his predictability, while God is known for his unpredictability, for the surprises with which he works. In life, let's be quick to embrace this reality rather than push it away. Face it—you cannot shove God into a box. He's way too big to fit into it! You need to simply be brave and courageous enough to let him surprise you and maybe, just maybe, you'll be the surprise waiting to happen in someone else's life.

6

Life-Jacket Theology

Staying Afloat in a Fallen World

Key Points

• *David sent for the lost Mephibosheth, just as God sent Christ to seek out and to save those who were lost.*
• *A life jacket, developed to keep you alive, is useless unless you wear it.*

As I alluded to in an earlier chapter, I have not always made the wisest decisions in my life, and like many people, I am still living with some of the consequences. Some of the things that happened to me were of my own doing and some were not. One could say that at times, I was splashing around in murky, shark-infested waters of sin, nearly losing my life in its ripples and waves on different occasions.

The ironic thing was that I was lost and didn't even know that I needed to be found. I had simply accepted that this is how life is and rolled with the punches. The awesome thing is that the reason I'm even writing this book is because in my early twenties my Savior came into view and a life jacket of sorts was thrown my way. It saved my life.

In the 2 Samuel 9, we meet a man named Mephibosheth. David asks, "Is there anyone still left of the house of Saul to whom I can show kindness for Jonathan's sake?" (verse 1). He learns from a servant, "There is still a son of Jonathan; he is crippled in both feet. . . . He is . . . in Lo-Debar" (verse 3). As we move through this story, I invite you to play the supporting role of Mephibosheth.

Mephibosheth was the grandson of King Saul and the son of Jonathan. He was the son of a prince, living in a desolate place called Lo-Debar, which literally means "a place of no pasture." To put it bluntly, the regional housing developers weren't waiting in line to snatch up all the land they could in Lo-Debar. It simply wasn't a very desirable place to live.

When he was younger, Mephibosheth had experienced a fall that crippled both his feet (2 Samuel 4:4). So he couldn't walk on his own. He was older now and forced to accept his condition and his unfortunate lot in life. What else could he do? It's safe to say that he would've anonymously perished without David's intentional intervention. We likely never would've heard or known of him if David had not graciously reached out to him and rescued him from his impossible situation.

David made the first move by sending someone to bring Mephibosheth to the royal place so he could be received and accepted. David sent for a lost Mephibosheth, just as God sent Christ to earth to seek out and save the lost, namely you and me.

Here David richly symbolized Christ, who later taught us, "In my Father's house are many rooms; if it were not so, I would have told you. I am going there to prepare a place for you. And if I go and prepare a place for you, I will come back and take you to be with me that you also may be where I am" (John 14:2-3).

Christ did indeed leave a perfect heaven, and he came to us, in this modern-day place of Lo-Debar. He did this in obedience and in honor of his relationship with his heavenly Father. In a similar way, we observe how David's actions were in honor of his friend Jonathan. David tells Mephibosheth, "I will surely show you kindness for the sake of your father Jonathan. I will restore to you all the land that belonged to your grandfather Saul, and you will always eat at my table" (2 Samuel 9:7). David had made an agreement with Jonathan earlier to show kindness and to protect his family. He remembered this and extended a lifeline to Mephibosheth. This was done, in large part, to honor this covenant he had made.

Just as Jesus Christ does for you and me, David provided for Mephibosheth's every need. He would now eat daily at the king's table and would receive the inheritance that belonged to him. We must fully understand and grasp that we are also sons and daughters of royalty. We also reside in a place of "no pasture." We live in a fallen, sinful world. Like Mephibosheth in Lo-Debar, we can consume or experience nothing that will truly satisfy us. In short, our thirst here will never be fully quenched.

Because of the fall of Adam, we live in a fallen world (see Romans 5:12). All of us have fallen in our sin. We can never walk a straight enough line through our own strength. We, like Mephibosheth, limp along and need to be picked up and rescued. We would also perish without an act of mercy. As lost sinners, we are ultimately helpless and often find ourselves feeling like Mephibosheth, as we too are far from home.

Be assured however, that God still meets the Mephibosheths of the world. God meets people who, like us, are spiritually disabled. Someone once said, "The very moment Eve bit the fruit, Jesus started packing his bags." Because of Jesus Christ, we are a grace-given people.

David restored Mephibosheth from a place of no pasture to a place of honor. As God's children, we also have been invited to dine as honorary guests and feast at his banquet. Remember too that David invited Mephibosheth into the king's family and adopted him as a king's son. This is precisely what God has done for all persons everywhere who believe in him and accept his love.

Consider someone you know who needs a life jacket. What shark-infested waters has that person been swimming in? Who do you know that's exhausted from swimming against the tide? Who is it that needs to be rescued from a dry, barren land? Perhaps you are struggling to stay afloat. Are you tired of grazing in a land of no pasture?

The life jacket was developed to keep people alive. But it is useless unless you wear it. During one particularly stressful time, I took my wife on a little surprise getaway. We traveled to a nearby lake and rented a boat. The idea was to get away from everything for a while. No phone, no noise, no responsibilities.

We were having a great, relaxing time out in the middle of the lake—until my wife realized that I wasn't wearing my life jacket. Why couldn't she relax? For good reason. She was anxious because I can't swim. She knew what the result could be if I fell into the water unprotected. I assured her that I'd be fine, but she wasn't convinced and insisted that I put the jacket on.

This is the same kind of anxiety and urgency we must have for persons who are unprotected from the shark-infested waters of sin. Like David to Mephibosheth and like Christ to our sinful world, God calls us to intercede and be lovingly persistent with those persons in our life who need to be fitted with the eternal life jacket. The covenant you've made with your Creator to "go and make disciples" is still binding. Will you be the one to throw a life jacket?

7

What's on the Menu?

Hunger and Thirst for Righteousness

Key Points

- *When we're mere spectators, we get out of shape, lazy, complacent.*
- *When we are babies, we need to be fed. As we grow, we feed ourselves. As we mature, we feed others.*

Here's a scene that many of us know very well. It's around noon on Thanksgiving Day, and we're eating our turkey, dressing, and pumpkin pie. We get to that point where we decline any more food because, instead of the turkey, we're the ones who are stuffed. We put up our hand to our host and assuredly say, "I'm so full I probably won't eat again until tomorrow." But some of the leftovers often remain on the table during the afternoon, and before you know it you are grazing again. A few hours later you devour a turkey sandwich and just one more "small" piece of pie with whipped topping.

We're reminded here that when we eat, we're only temporarily full. Jesus shares with us how we can permanently be filled in a spiritual sense with him: "Blessed are those who hunger and thirst for righteousness, for they will be filled" (Matthew 5:6). In the context of this verse, to hunger means to have a starving spirit. It is having a desperate hunger for the things of God. It's saying, "If I don't have it, I can't make it." It indicates a deep hunger for all of righteousness and for all of what Christ has to offer, not just little tidbits.

So, what is righteousness? We generally think of it as doing good things and helping others around us. As we go through life, we are faced with appeal after appeal for help. Many times we do help, which brings us a sense of satisfaction. We feel that our good deeds somehow make us more acceptable before God. While it's good to help others, it is not true righteousness.

In the Bible, righteousness simply means to *be right* and to *do right*—to be good and to do good for the right reasons and with the right motives. From this, however, a problem arises. Paul reminds us, "There is no one righteous, not even one. . . . For all have sinned and fall short of the glory of God" (Romans 3:10, 23). How can we then make sense of this?

What is being said here is that God alone is righteous and perfectly good. You and I are not righteous; all our efforts will fall short. How is it then that we can become righteous? We must simply hunger for it. God takes our hunger for righteousness and counts it as righteousness. In essence, he credits our account with it.

When my boys were really young, I would often be found in the backyard, pitching ball to them. I knew it was impossible for them to hit it every time. Actually, if they hit maybe three out of ten, it was an accomplishment. If I saw them wanting to give up too soon, I would assure them that no one hits the ball every time and encourage them to keep trying. In the end, if they really tried hard, even though they whiffed at more balls than they hit, I would still credit them with a job well done and maybe go get them ice cream cones.

Logically, this makes no sense. Here were my children with a 30-percent success rate, and I was rewarding their effort. Likewise, God intercedes for us and counts us as righteous because of our hunger and our desire for him. He doesn't expect us to be perfect; *we* often expect us to be perfect.

If we hunger, we will be blessed. Being blessed literally means that we will obtain a deep, internal joy and satisfaction that cannot be swayed by the external conditions around us. Unlike our temporary Thanksgiving dinner, we will experience a feeling of being filled permanently in a lasting, spiritual sense.

Let's think about thirst. Our bodies are about 80 percent water. As you may have discovered, when you don't drink enough, your body lets you know. You get a headache and generally start to feel miserable. Spiritually, when we're not quenching ourselves with the things of Christ, similar things happen. We become short-tempered, irritable, and resentful. A sort of spiritual dehydration sets in that also leaves us feeling lethargic and exhausted.

Avoiding this spiritual dehydration and remaining quenched in Christ requires action on our part. A few years ago, one of my sons ran on the cross-country team. Our family often went to the meets, and we noticed that the same thing happened at the end of every race. When the runners were finished, they'd gulp down water. Why were they the ones drinking? I would have gotten funny looks if, as a spectator, I was standing there gulping the water. The runners were the ones who had been generating a thirst. They had been the active participants in running the race and naturally were thirstier than any spectator would've been.

When we're only spectators, we quickly get out of shape, lazy, and complacent. In doing so, we don't generate an intense appetite for food or a strong thirst for water within our bodies. It's only when we have a true passion, a yearning, and a goal in mind that we will stretch ourselves, go the extra mile, and become hungry and thirsty. We must simply choose to put on our running shoes and get out on the course.

Scripture exhorts us to *crave* the things of God: "Like new-born babies, crave pure spiritual milk, so that by it you may grow up in your salvation" (1 Peter 2:2). We are to desire and long for the things of God as intensely as a baby desires milk. To those of us with children, this is a vivid picture. I remember how unsettled and unsatisfied my boys were before they drank the milk and how peaceful and content they were afterward. Are you like this with the things of God? Are you even hungry for him, let alone craving him? Is your life unsettled and unsatisfied when you don't feed on him?

As a pastor, I invariably hear people talk of how they left their church because they weren't "being fed." When we are babies, we need to be fed. But as we begin to grow, we are able to feed ourselves. And as we mature, we become the feeders. Do you feed others, or are you still a baby that needs to be spoon-fed?

When you sit down at a restaurant, often the first question you are asked is, "What would you like to drink?" As you meet God each day at the table of his mercy, what is it that you would like to drink and eat? What might you offer him from your menu? Do you find yourself spiritually bloated and left with that heavy feeling from the bad, fast-food diet of the world around you? Or are you in shape and refueling yourself with the pure living water of Christ?

When one of my boys gets a snack, you can be sure that his brothers want the same thing he has. It looks good, and they immediately desire it. I wonder if the same could be said about us. Are the items on the menu we offer healthy and appealing? Do others want what we have to offer? Can God receive what we have to offer? Is what we have so irresistible that others can't wait to have it as well? Are we offering the free, pure, living water as a menu item?

As a "certified spiritual florist," you will remember that flowers need water and that bouquets are made of numerous flowers. As you're offering these bouquets to God and others, make sure they're watered daily.

A friend of mine is a retired truck driver who has eaten in his share of restaurants and diners during his years out on the road. He made a good analogy when he said that for years, he would go into the diner and not even look at a menu. Every time it was the same order: cheeseburger and fries. He was so comfortable with his cheeseburger and fries that he never bothered to consider anything else. He feared that maybe he had become this way in his spiritual life as well. Same old, same old, predictable and bland. How about you? Is it time you tried something new? What can you do for your Creator today?

We can risk disease by drinking from this world's stagnant, mosquito- and algae-infested pond. Or we can take big swallows where the water is fresh and disease is obsolete.

God desires to satisfy your hunger and to quench your thirst once and for all. Will you give him your appetites and allow him to fill you?

8

The Picture of Perfection

It's Who You Know

Key Points

• *We need to get out of our ivory towers, get our knees stained with prayer, and get our hands dirty as we cultivate a personal relationship with Jesus Christ.*
• *When we're healed by forgiveness for our sins, we can live in the present, set apart from the bondage of a sinful lifestyle.*

Epaphras was a pastor of the small church in the town and region of Colossae. He was troubled by the increasing amount of false teaching creeping into the church. He needed to confront it and had asked Paul to help him by sharing some words of exhortation and truth. Paul's words are what we know today as his letter to the Colossians. A question he addressed is one we still ask today: who is Jesus, really?

Someone once asked, is he our Monarch or simply our mascot, our Creator or our convenience? If someone were to ask you, what would you say?

Paul writes about the supremacy of Christ, "He is the image of the invisible God, the firstborn over all creation" (Colossians 1:15). *Image* here means the exact image—the very person of God. It means a mark or figure stamped on something, a precise reproduction.

When most people took photos with film cameras, they'd sometimes have the film developed to get doubles of each photo. The duplicate was not a mere resemblance but an exact copy. Paul is saying that Jesus is this picture of perfection—the perfect revelation from God. We know that God is humanly invisible, but Jesus reveals God to the world as an exact image. By his life and example, Jesus has shown us who God is and what God is like.

Paul wrote this letter because of his and the church's concern with the false teaching of Gnosticism, which claimed that Jesus was not the only way to God but simply one of many ways. Many people today still agree with this, and the prevalent belief is that there are many paths to God. But Peter preached, "Salvation is found in no one else, for there is no other name under heaven given to men by which we must be saved" (Acts 4:12).

What the Colossians needed to understand and what we need to understand today is that the one, true God is not located in a far-away galaxy, leaving us to fend for ourselves and to clumsily stumble through life. God loves all people so much that he has shown us exactly who he is, what he is like, and how to reach him. Jesus alone is the mediator and precise image of God: "For God was pleased to have all his fullness dwell in him" (Colossians 1:19). No other good teacher or holy prophet could have on his résumé "I am the way and the truth and the life. No one comes to the Father except through me" (John 14:6).

The teaching of Gnosticism also claims that the way to God is primarily through reasoning and intellectual ability. It was thought that a person needed a certain amount of secret religious knowledge to gain God's acceptance and favor. One needed to know how to act, how to dress, and most importantly the right religious words to say. This brought a false sense of safety and security to the Colossians.

Human behavior doesn't seem to have changed much, as many of us live this way today, with a sort of comfy-couch Christianity. We feel if we look pretty on Sunday morning and know enough key words and phrases, we can get by without being challenged.

The truth is that God never has and never will receive and redeem persons because they know about him, about religion, or about religious buzzwords. Christians today need to confront this temptation of dress-up Christianity. We need to get out of our ivory towers, get our knees stained with prayer, and get our hands dirty as we cultivate our personal relationship with Jesus Christ.

When one of my sons was younger, he asked me if I knew the famous basketball player Lebron James. I said that I did, much to his delight. I wondered why he was so excited about this, and as our conversation continued I discovered why. He thought that I knew James personally. I then had to clarify that I knew *of* him but had never spent any time with him to really *know* him and to discover what he's like personally. I then explained that just because you know *about* someone doesn't mean you really *know* him or her on a personal basis.

In your spiritual life, do you simply know who Christ is, or do you honestly know him on a personal, intimate level?

Paul called Jesus "the firstborn over all creation" (Colossians 1:15). Here *firstborn* means priority, superiority, and supremacy. It indicates how he existed before all of creation as the Supreme Being of the universe and how all of creation is his heritage, including little old you. "The Son is the radiance of God's glory and the exact representation of his being, sustaining all things by his powerful word. After he had provided purification for sins, he sat down at the right hand of the Majesty in heaven" (Hebrews 1:3).

Imagine you're sitting at an expensive, elaborate gourmet steakhouse. This establishment is known far and wide as "the place" for steaks. It is the kind of place where they are so confident of their steaks that there is not a bottle of A-1 steak sauce to be found. It's clearly understood that it would be rude and even insulting to ask for steak sauce. After all, why would you need it when the original is that good?

Spiritually, the same is true with all of us. When we attempt to add anything to the standard, it is contrary to Scripture and an insult to our Creator. There is none other who can bring us near to God and no other lifestyle to follow in reaching God. Jesus Christ can never simply be our mascot. He is the majesty of the universe, who came into the world to establish an intentional personal relationship with each of us and to save us from the power of evil.

Only one being in the history of time could've done this. "Since the children have flesh and blood, he too shared in their humanity so that by his death he might destroy him who holds the power of death—that is, the devil—and free those who all their lives were held in slavery by their fear of death" (Hebrews 2:14-15).

First, *Jesus did this in becoming a man.* He was 100-percent divine in nature, yet he willingly chose to partner with us in our human nature. He loved us so much that he would pay the ultimate price to deliver us. He would humble himself and literally leave heaven to do this. Clearly he couldn't die for us unless he was first born.

Second, *Jesus did this in his death.* All of us die. We die because of sin; because we are short of perfection. Death is the result of sin. If we are to live forever, sin and death have to be taken care of and removed. This is what this perfect Christ has done for an imperfect you and me in his death.

Third, *Jesus destroyed the power of Satan over sin and death.*

Make no mistake, there is a battle waging for our souls. The word *destroy* means "to bring to nothing." Christ has destroyed Satan's power. In Christ, we no longer are slaves to sin and its guilt, nor to death. We are instead delivered from death because Christ has broken Satan's power over death. We're not only healed by the forgiveness of our past sins, but we also can live in the present, set apart from the bondage of a sinful lifestyle.

Finally, *Jesus delivers us from the fear of death*. In Christ, there is no need to fear death. Why? Because we will never die. When our bodies stop working, we will not taste death but will be in his presence quicker than the blink of an eye. Our physical existence is a mere drop in the ocean of our life's existence. There is no death and condemnation for the Christian believer. There is nothing to fear. Death has indeed been swallowed up in victory.

A familiar Christmas song reminds us of these great truths:

> God rest ye merry gentlemen, let nothing you dismay
> Remember Christ our Savior was born on Christmas day
> To save us all from Satan's power when we were gone
>   astray
> O tidings of comfort and joy

All of this brings into focus the picture of perfection—God coming to a sinful world. Nothing can substitute what Christ has already done for us and nothing can compare to us being delivered and rescued from a hopeless death to an eternal life.

One of the most familiar verses in all of Scripture is the one Jesus shared with an inquiring Nicodemus one dark night. Jesus told this Pharisee, who was also a member of the Jewish ruling council, "God so loved the world that he gave his one and only Son, that whoever believes in him shall not perish but have eternal life" (John 3:16). Thank you, Jesus, for coming to this sinful world and for being our picture of perfection.

9

A Tale of Two Offerings

Matters of the Heart

Key Points

• *God accepts our Sunday morning worship only if our lives demonstrate our faith the rest of the week.*
• *We have a relationship with God through our hearts, not our heads—not by what we do, but by what our motives are.*
• *Our Creator gave us the gifts of life, hope, and salvation. He's also planned out the good works for which we were uniquely created.*

You've hit another milestone birthday, and your spouse has decided to remind you of this by throwing a surprise party. You and I have been friends for a few years, and so when I get my invitation, I make a note of it on my calendar and plan to attend. The days leading up to your party are hectic for me and on the actual day of it, I'm flat-out swamped. Somehow,

I do manage to remember your party and arrive, albeit a little late. When I get there, my heart sinks because everyone else is giving you a birthday gift. It obviously slipped my mind to get you a gift, so I quickly rush next door to the convenience store. I scan the shelves for an entire minute and hurriedly grab a bag of chips and a king-size candy bar. When I come back to your party, you smile, thank me for coming, and gladly receive my gift, sort of. It's obvious that I didn't spend a great deal of time picking your gift out, unless I can convince you that every time I think of salt and vinegar potato chips, you readily come to my mind in an endearing way. You know my gift wasn't from the heart and, quite frankly, it does make a difference.

Consider the story of Cain and Abel (see Genesis 4). Cain is the firstborn son of Adam and Eve and grows up to become a farmer. He goes out into his fields one day to harvest some of his crops. As he does so, he decides that it's probably about time to give an offering to God. So he grabs some of his wheat and corn and gives it as an offering to the Lord. The Lord considers Cain's offering and decides it's unacceptable.

At first this doesn't make much sense. After all, being a farmer and giving a grain offering would've been very common. Looking deeper, it seems it wasn't the content of the offering that God rejected, but rather the heart of the person making it. "On Cain and his offering [God] did not look with favor" (Genesis 4:5). Clearly, Cain had a deeper problem of the heart. It appears that his sacrifice was more of an attempt to appease God than to please God.

Many of us today feel that we're doing our duty and doing God a favor by going to church every Sunday, hoping that this two-hour sacrifice of our time will somehow appease God. It's fascinating how we act and speak however we want from Monday through Saturday and excuse our behavior because "Hey, what more do you want? At least I'm in church on Sunday morning!"

We live selfishly, giving little regard to our neighbors, to the hurting, and to the needy. We have very little time or no time at all for prayer or Bible study. Often the only time we remember God is when we want something from him.

The ultimate success of any church will never be based merely on what happens within its walls on Sunday mornings. It will be based on what happens each week in our communities from Monday through Saturday. We don't *go* to church; we *are* the church!

The offering of our time and ourselves can never become a mere duty. It is an offering of worship. God accepts our Sunday morning worship only if our lives demonstrate our faith the rest of the week. This is where Cain failed. He believed that his duty of worship would be good enough for God and that the rest of his life and actions wouldn't matter. When he discovered that his worship, his partial offering, was not acceptable to God, he became angry.

It's like the sixteen-year-old son who doesn't get his way. Picture the scene as his dad is sitting in the living room, reading the newspaper. The suddenly mild-mannered son walks into the room and says, "Dad, I love you."

Being a seasoned veteran, Dad says, "Okay, what do you want?"

"C'mon, Dad, I just wanted to tell you I love you and that I think you're great."

"Well, thank you very much."

"Oh, and by the way, can I borrow the car tonight? I'm going to a party."

"Son, you know I need the car tonight," Dad says.

So, what does the son do? He goes stomping out of the room, quickly forgetting how much he loves his dad and what a great guy he is. His worship was only a way to appease his father and an attempt to selfishly get what he wanted.

Cain approached God with an offering. God, seeing that his

heart wasn't right, couldn't accept it. Instead of repenting and changing, Cain stormed off in an angry, jealous rage.

Abel's offering is different. Why was God willing to accept it? Because "Abel brought fat portions from some of the first-born of his flock" (4:4). Bringing the fat portions caused the Lord to look at Abel and his offering with favor. Abel's offering was acceptable to God because it was honorable and sincere. Abel knew he could not appease God, so he made a sacrifice that reflected his heart's desire to follow the Lord. From his heart, Abel gave not the leftovers but the fat portions, the best of his best. It was done as an obedient act of worship and was therefore honored and accepted.

God didn't have a problem with Cain's offering. The problem was with the one offering it. Cain could make all of the sacrifices he wanted to, but until his heart was right, he could never have a true relationship with God.

We sometimes tend to think that God loves our mere church involvement. We teach Sunday school, work in the nursery, or lead singing. Some, like me, even preach from the pulpit. As we do these things, we hope that all of it will somehow make us more acceptable to God.

But in fact God has already been appeased. Jesus Christ bought and paid for our salvation some two thousand years ago on the cross. Our response must be the same as Abel's. The only way we can have a real relationship with God is through our hearts, not our heads. It's not so much *what* we do, but rather who we are and our motives for doing what we do. It doesn't matter what we sacrifice for God. If our heart isn't right with him, he cannot and will not accept our offering. But if our heart is in the right place, any offering we give will be received as a fresh, pleasing aroma to him.

As you consider this tale of two offerings, ponder whether you give limited or unlimited offerings to your Creator. For several years, our church welcomed a missionary family who had moved into our area to serve the Lord in mission aviation work. We knew they would be with us for just a short time, and after two years or so they talked about having the desire to move to "Boondocksville," Alaska, to serve in a similar capacity there. They were originally from the deep south of Texas and in their words were "tired of hot."

At one point during their ongoing time of waiting and seeking, my wife, Jocelyn, and I had a conversation with them about our family's plans for summer vacation. We told them that we were looking forward to taking our three boys to Florida for a fun-filled week of sun and sand. They just shook their heads in disagreement and exclaimed in a southern drawl, "Too hot, way too hot!" They mentioned again how tired they were of hot weather and how hopeful they were for a placement in Alaska.

Guess where this wonderful family is faithfully serving the Lord today—hot, sunny Florida! They very well may have said, "God, we're willing, if we can go to Alaska." This is a really good offering, but it's a *limited* offering. In the end, they were obedient enough to give an unlimited offering by declaring, "God, we're willing, period." This family now knows it's not *where* they go, it's *why* they go.

With any offering, it's not *what* we give, it's *why* we give. Limited offerings cannot be fully received by God, because they're not fully given by us.

As you reflect on these things, ask yourself if you are offering your time, talent, and future to God as an unlimited offering and with wild abandon. Or are you playing it close to the vest and missing out on God's best blessings for your life? What kind of giver are you?

To be good *givers* of offerings, we must also know how to be good *receivers* of gifts. I can't offer you a refreshing, cool drink of water unless I've first allowed my glass to be filled. It's only when I've smelled the wonderful aromas of God's fresh bouquets for myself that I can fully share it and pass it along to you.

A young man was graduating from college. For months he had admired a sports car and hinted heavily to his father that this would be a great gift. On the morning of his graduation, his father called him into his study just to tell him how proud he was and how much he loved him. He then handed his son a gift box containing a beautiful, leather-bound Bible. Angry and disappointed, the young man threw it to the floor and stormed out of the house.

Several years passed, and the son received word of his father's ill health. Before he could get home, his father died. When the son arrived, he began looking through his father's papers and quickly found the Bible. As he picked it up, a car key dropped from the back of it. It had a tag with the dealer's name, the day it could be picked up, and the words "paid in full" written on it.

How many times have you rejected your heavenly Father's gifts simply because they weren't packaged as you expected? A gift is something that cannot be earned but is freely given. As Paul wrote, "The wages of sin is death, but the gift of God is eternal life in Christ Jesus our Lord" (Romans 6:23).

I wonder how many of you reading this book asked to be born. How many said, "Hey, Mom and Dad, could I please be born now?" None of us asked to be born, yet here we are. How many of you demanded that Christ die on the cross for your sins? Your very life up until this moment and your life from here forward is a gift in the purest form.

Paul summed it up well: "For it is by grace you have been saved, through faith—and this is not from yourselves, it is the gift of God—not by works, so that no one can boast. For we are God's workmanship, created in Christ Jesus to do good works, which God prepared in advance for you to do" (Ephesians 2:8-10).

Your Creator gave you the gifts of life, hope, and salvation. Incredibly, he also planned out the good works, that is, your specific ministry, which you were uniquely created and gifted to do.

The Alaska-Florida family was specifically gifted for their

task. You are also specifically gifted for yours. Think how arrogant it is to "size up" the gifts of the Giver and decline them because they aren't what was expected. We wouldn't think of doing this with a gift from a friend or loved one. In refusing God's gift, we are in essence calling the shots and telling him what we want. This dangerous role reversal nurtures a dysfunctional relationship. When we determine that we are the god of something we didn't create, disaster awaits.

A friend of mine designs and builds small tractors. He knows the literal nuts and bolts of the tractors he works on. The minute I decide to tell him how to fix them, or if I tell a CEO how to run the company he's built from the ground up, I'm clearly out of line. The same is true with each of us and our Creator. Have you ever done this in your life? Are you presently doing it?

When the son received the gift of the Bible in our earlier story, what did he do with his gift? He threw it away and didn't accept it. The irony is that it was there the entire time. This is also the picture of your Father and his gifts to you.

Peter tells early church members—and us—to "use whatever gift [you have] received to serve others, faithfully administering God's grace" (1 Peter 4:10). At Christmastime or at a birthday party, we don't know exactly what's inside the gift with our name on it. We must first receive it, then unwrap it, and then use it.

Remember, the ultimate gift God offers is eternal life. Have you received this gift? Have you unwrapped it, or is it still on the shelf? Will you ultimately live it out with someone today and share its sweet aroma?

10

Emergency Spiritual Technicians

Workers for the Plentiful Harvest

Key Points

• *The Lord's call should be the primary seed of the soil of your life.*
• *Jesus taught that it's too late to spread his aroma to the dead. We are to focus on those persons who are physically living but spiritually dying.*
• *Many Christians have the best of intentions, but they do very little about it.*

As you settle down in your favorite chair with your hot beverage and a good book, you hear a siren wailing in the distance. As the ambulance comes closer, the sound becomes louder and then fades again as it moves along to its destination.

We are all very grateful for emergency medical technicians,

who give of their time and energies in this life-giving way. When someone's in trouble, they drop everything and respond immediately. It's not a time for laziness or excuses. The need is urgent and the response must be also.

Spiritually, we need this same kind of urgency. There is a world around us full of hurting persons. Many people have great needs, and as believers we have the cure. Believers can show these troubled souls how to be saved.

How, then, can we become the "emergency spiritual technicians" whom so many desperately need?

Jesus and his disciples were walking along the road when two men began talking to them. To one of the men, Jesus said, "Follow me." But the man replied, "Lord, first let me go and bury my father." Jesus said, "Let the dead bury their own dead, but you go and proclaim the kingdom of God" (Luke 9:59-60).

We see here how Christ calls for an immediate obedience, even when it doesn't make sense. We also see how Jesus kept talking to him even after the man hesitated. Jesus didn't want this man's logical reasoning to delay his launch into the harvest field. Instead, he urgently wanted this man to become a preacher of the gospel.

Christ has chosen you to be an invaluable part of carrying out his mission. How do you respond when the Holy Spirit comes to you? What excuses or hesitations immediately arise?

Every person is of great value to Jesus. Wherever you are planted, the Lord's call is to be the primary seed of the soil of your life.

God called the man in Luke, and yet he hesitated. It's important to note here that his hesitation was legitimate. He was concerned about caring for his father. It seems his father was already dead, or maybe he was close to death. So why the prodding by Jesus? What was he trying to teach this man? It appears the man's problem was one of divided attention. When he heard God's call, he immediately looked at his situation and couldn't see another solution. He didn't completely say no, but neither did he assuredly say yes. He made a partial commitment and left the impression that as soon as this situation was handled, he would follow Jesus. But Jesus demanded that he act now and not wait. He saw through the man's partial commitment. Whether it's our job, family, or money, there will always be something to point to that can delay our immediate service to him.

Jesus, though, demands our first fruits and an immediate response coupled with a keen sense of urgency. You may say, "C'mon, Jesus refused to give this man time to bury the dead!" Jesus was simply saying that because the need is so great and because it's too late to spread his aroma to the dead, we are to focus instead on those who are physically living but spiritually dying. Jesus implied that nothing more can be done for the dead, but the living can still be reached and saved. This is why the hour is urgent.

Just as Christ calls for immediate obedience, he also calls for focused, intentional obedience. He says, "The harvest is plentiful, but the workers are few. Ask the Lord of the harvest, therefore, to send out workers into his harvest field" (Luke 10:2). And he tells those who go, "Do not take a purse or bag or sandals; and do not greet anyone on the road" (verse 4). What does Jesus mean here? He means that within our urgent obedience, we are to trust him first and foremost. If he calls us to something, he will provide for us and sustain us, whether our need is money, food, housing, clothing, or one of a hundred other things.

Soon after I became a pastor, my family's financial situation became strained, to put it mildly. Jocelyn and I were living in an eight-hundred-square-foot house and parenting three boys, ages four, two, and four months. Jocelyn was a stay-at-home mom and could no longer contribute financially to the family. My beginning pastor's salary only stretched so far.

Having never been in financial need, we were in uncharted territory. We never knew how to ask for assistance and yet we found ourselves at a desperate point where we needed help. Reluctantly, we signed up with the Women, Infants, and Children public assistance program, which generously provided many of the necessities our little guys needed.

I remember how humbling it was when we went through the grocery lines and saw people's judgmental reactions as Jocelyn handed over the food vouchers. At one point, all I could do was cry. In retrospect however, once we got past our pride, we now recall those years as some of the best years of our lives. We realize now that it was an integral time of learning and of substantial spiritual growth for both of us. We've actually thanked God for allowing us to experience those circumstances. He is indeed *Jehovah Jirah*—our Provider.

Jesus reminds us here that worrying about things takes too much away from the precious time we've been given to minister in his name. Also, we're not to waste a lot of time in idle chitchat and needless conversation. We're not to talk only about the weather, the sports scores, or any other insignificant, everyday events. Our conversation should focus on his purposes and his kingdom.

The urgency in these passages is so clear and intense that it almost seems insensitive and somewhat offensive. We feel Jesus pushing us to a deeper understanding of the urgency he feels when it comes to lost souls. How often have you heard yourself saying, "I was going to do that for . . ." "I thought of being there for . . ." "I'll obey God's call right after . . ." "I had every intention of . . ." "If I wouldn't have been so busy, I would've . . ." and the list goes on and on.

It's been my experience that many Christians live with an embarrassing passivity. In other words, we have the best of intentions but do very little about it. We can be lazy Christians. We're living in a world that desperately needs the love of Christ. The problem is that most of us seem preoccupied, uninterested, and generally unconcerned about the urgency of his call in our lives.

But these verses, and many others, remind us of the priority of the gospel message and the urgency with which it needs to be shared.

Do you live your life with this intense urgency? Are you quick to say no to God's call and yes to your immediate needs? If so, why? How excited are you today to make his mission the number-one priority in your life? With whom will you be urgent and help to rescue?

11

Suggestions or Commandments?

Be the Aroma of Christ

Key Points

• *One reason some things happen to you is so to help you identify with other's situations and better minister to them.*
• *Rather than waiting for something big to happen, be faithful and bloom wherever you're planted.*

A friend of mine unexpectedly found himself in a bed in the emergency room of our local hospital. As he was thinking about his own condition, he looked up and saw a familiar face. This younger man's mother was on another floor at the same hospital, suffering from the effects of cancer. He had overheard that my friend was in the emergency room and sought him out. This "spiritual florist" simply talked with my friend for a few moments and then quietly prayed a meaningful prayer. This then inspired my friend to commit himself to a more active prayer life of his own. It took five minutes to create a memory that my friend will never forget.

James wrote, "Do not merely listen to the word, and so deceive yourselves. Do what it says" (1:22). Clearly, it's one thing to listen to something or to read about something, and it's something quite more to do what it says.

Jocelyn had been waking up a little earlier than usual to start out her day with some uninterrupted "quiet time" with God. She had been getting up great for a while, but like all of us, she sort of started the habit of hitting the snooze button again. One night she asked the Lord not to let this happen again the next morning. She really wanted and needed this time alone with him, so she earnestly prayed that he would "get her up."

At six the next morning, she reached over and shut off that annoying sound of the alarm clock and started drifting off back into la-la land. At 6:01 a.m., a vehicle went past our house, and a man yelled out its window, and I quote, "Get uuup!" This had never happened before and hasn't happened since. As she laughed to herself, she rolled out of bed and started the coffee, amazed once again at her Creator. She could've simply listened to that wild man's voice and stayed in bed, but she chose to do what it said.

How do you read, hear, and listen to God's Word? Do you view the Scriptures as mere suggestions or as commandments to be lived out? The general tendency is to view and accept the Word in light of how we feel about it and how it fits us within our situation. We often subconsciously try to figure out how we can justify our actions by "twisting" the Scriptures so that they serve us. We need to understand very clearly, however, that Scripture doesn't serve us; we are to serve it. We can think or read or talk about things all day long. But, if we don't ultimately act, we're pretty foolish. The letter of James says that living this way is as foolish as a man who couldn't even remember his own face right after looking at it in the mirror.

I have several friends who are medical doctors. They talk about how it's not uncommon for persons to come back to see them for a follow-up appointment and not be improving. The doctor will ask if they took the medication as it was prescribed to them. Often the patients will admit that after a whole day of taking the medication, they thought they would just quit. In effect, they took the advice of the doctor as a suggestion. Little wonder why they're still sick.

Like many of you probably do, I struggle with high cholesterol. My doctor told me very plainly that in order to control it, I must get to know two words very well: oatmeal and exercise. I could disagree, or take a pill that would begin to kill my liver, or I could choose to do what the doctor says.

This is important to grasp because, as James 1:22 tells us, when it comes to the Word, we deceive ourselves when we decide not to do what it says. This brings to mind the story of the nephew who had a rich, elderly uncle. The uncle wanted to make sure that his nephew received a college education, so he set up a college fund for him. This fund would take care of all his academic and living expenses as long as he remained in college. Long after his uncle had died, the nephew was sixty-three years old and had twenty college degrees to his name. The uncle's provision had allowed him never to work a day in life. How useless! He had all of that knowledge and never put any of it to use.

Scriptures are not suggestions! I'm a firm believer that strong Christians rarely sit back and simply let things happen to them. Strong, mature believers make it a point to go out and happen to the world around them. A good friend of mine is a middle-school basketball coach who understands this. He had a new player on his team one year who had participated in all of the off-season camps and open gyms. Shortly before the season began, he broke a bone and was out for the season.

My friend could've very easily paid less attention to this young man. After all, he wouldn't be scoring one single point for the team.

However, my friend didn't ignore him or consider him useless at all. Instead, he sat down and wrote out a very encouraging, inspiring, and spiritual letter, offering his thoughts and prayers to both this player and his parents. He actually took the opportunity to add much more to the relationship by reaching out and sending a spiritual bouquet their way.

When Scripture says to
Love your neighbor as yourself—Do what it says!
Be kind and forgiving—Do what it says!
Make the most of every opportunity—Do what it says!
Be the aroma and the fragrance of Christ—Do what it says!

The fact is that your life as a Christian is doing one of two things each and every day: either *clarifying* the gospel message or *confusing* the gospel message. Which does your life do? When persons look at the way you live, do they say, "Alright, I get it—that's what it's like to be a Christian." Or do they say, "Hmm, if that's what it's like to be a Christian, I'm not so sure."

As long as we're living, we each have a job to do. As we constantly strive to do what the Word says, we do it best by recognizing the necessity of operating and partnering together as believers. We must realize and celebrate that we all have different gifts, one not being more important or more valuable than another. Some of us preach from a pulpit with words while others preach in the workplace with actions. Some of us like to visit the sick while others make meals for young mothers. Some of us simply smile and have a good attitude while others of us are patient and gentle as we change yet another diaper. It's been said that the man who steadies the ladder at the bottom is just as important as the man at the top. All kinds of spiritual gifts are clearly needed!

Just as we have differing gifts, we also have different assignments. We express our giftedness as we live out our days, by completing our assignments. Here are just a few everyday examples:

- One assignment is *encouragement*. Consider the

sandhill crane. These large birds, which fly great distances across continents, have three remarkable qualities: (1) They rotate leadership. No one bird stays out in front all the time. (2) They choose leaders that can handle turbulence. (3) All during the time one bird is leading, the rest are honking their affirmation. This is a good model for us as believers. We need servant leaders who can handle turbulence. But most of all we need a climate in which we are all honking encouragement.

• Another assignment is to provide *comfort*—a listening ear, a pat on the back, or a little gift for no reason. This is ministry at its finest. Paul reminds us "to comfort those in any trouble with the comfort we ourselves have received from God" (2 Corinthians 1:4). Troubles happen for a reason. One is so that we can specifically identify with another's situation and better minister to them because of it.

• One last assignment is *prayer*. We read of how Epaphras, the pastor of the Colossian church, prayed. Paul says, "He is always wrestling in prayer for you, that you may stand firm in all the will of God, mature and fully assured" (Colossians 4:12). Do you pray like this for the persons in your church, your workplace, or your home? Consider picking five people within your circle of influence and become exhausted "wrestling in prayer" for them. They need your intentional prayers of intercession just as much as you need the prayers of others.

In the 1960s TV sitcom *The Andy Griffith Show*, Aunt Bee comes to live with Sheriff Andy Taylor and his son, Opie, after the death of Andy's wife. They thought that maybe Aunt Bee could bring that missing feminine touch. Opie wasn't impressed, so Andy tried to help them bond by inviting her to go fishing and frog catching. She fails miserably at these things and later with trying to throw a football.

One night, Aunt Bee talks Andy into taking her to the bus station. Opie hears her crying and guesses that she is leaving. He then runs out and exclaims, "We can't let her go, Pa, she needs us. Besides, she can't even catch frogs, bait a hook, or throw a football. Pa, we've got to take care of her, or she'll never make it."

We know that it takes one tree beside one tree beside one tree to create a forest. Together they provide many purposes and produce life-giving shelter, food, and oxygen. As we exist one person beside one person beside one person, we too can produce life-giving effects in a spiritual way. Instead of waiting for something "big" to happen, we can decide to be faithful and bloom wherever we're planted.

It's true that most of life is made up of small, seemingly insignificant events. It is in the phone calls, chance meetings, and mundane Mondays that the seeds are to be planted and that the aromas are to be shared. Just as it takes a lot of individual pieces of sand to form a beach, it takes more than one or two flowers to form a bouquet. Pray that your example would be observed by someone who will then pass it on to someone else and on and on and on.

Whose life will you touch beginning this week? Devise a plan and complete the assignment! Live simply. Love generously. Care deeply. Speak kindly.

It's been said that we make a living by what we get, but we make a life by what we give away. "But thanks be to God, who always leads us in triumphal procession in Christ and through us spreads everywhere the fragrance of the knowledge of him" (2 Corinthians 2:14).

Be the aroma!

Study Guide

Week One - Read introduction and chapter one.

Scripture readings: Ecclesiastes 11:1-4; 1 Corinthians 3:6-9; 2 Corinthians 2:14-15; Ephesians 2:10

1. Who are the "town grumps" in your life? Ask God to bring a name or two to mind and list them below. Perhaps it's a family member, neighbor, or co-worker. Pray for them daily and seek God's guidance on how to become a "certified spiritual florist."

2. Read 2 Corinthians 2:14-15. What is the aroma of Christ?

3. Bruce writes in chapter one, "You can now choose to live with this wonderful fragrance coming forth and oozing from within you." How would our lives be changed if we truly lived this life that Bruce is describing? How would our relationships with others change?

4. Reflect on this day and the previous weeks. Were your days full of busyness, or did you allow yourself the grace needed to pursue the God-initiated interruptions?

5. To fully take advantage of each day and to begin giving bouquets to the living, our attitudes must be reshaped and molded by Christ. Take time to humble yourself before the Lord and ask for his help to shape your attitude.

Week Two - Read chapters two and three.

Scripture readings: Matthew 5:7; John 4:14; 8:1-11; 2 Corinthians 8:10-12; 2 Timothy 1:16-18

1. Does God really expect us to be rock droppers? What about those "dirty" people? How can we show mercy to the vilest offenders?

2. Imagine yourself in the same spot as the adulterous woman. The arms are raised, the rocks are aimed, and then Jesus intervenes and takes away the punishment. How do you feel?

3. Look again at the story of the woman at the well (John 4:7-29). Notice what happens when someone is forgiven and encouraged. Yet it is much easier to judge and condemn. Talk about the ways in which our witness is damaged when we do not extend grace.

4. Bruce writes of concern, compassion, and commitment as traits of sponge squeezers. Of those three, which is the most difficult for you to show to others and why?

5. Look back at your list of persons from week one. What rocks do you need to drop? What dungeons need to be visited? List the steps needed to be taken in order to restore and refresh these persons?

Week Three - Read chapters four and five.

Scripture readings: Isaiah 55:8-11; John 13:34-35; Acts 23:12-24; 2 Timothy 4:9-21

1. We live in a hurried world. We want our food fast and our sermons short. We even want our relationships to be easy and on our terms. Think closely about Paul's words to Timothy. If a friend came to you in need, what would it take for you to drop everything and to "come before winter"?

2. Bruce writes about going the extra mile for someone. Is this simply an issue of priorities? If not, what else is involved?

3. Reflect on your own faith journey. Take some time to recall the people God has used to surprise you and to show you his love. Were these surprises freely received or hard to accept?

4. Look again at the list of persons from week one. Continue to pray for those listed and for the strength needed to go the extra mile with them.

Week Four - Read chapters six and seven.

Scripture readings: 2 Samuel 9:1-13; Matthew 5:6; John 14:1-6; Romans 3:10, 23; 1 Peter 2:2

1. When were you like Mephibosheth?

2. When have you been like David? What is keeping you from becoming a David to someone else?

3. Bruce defines *blessed* as obtaining "a deep, internal joy and satisfaction that cannot be swayed by the external conditions around us." Do you agree with this definition? Why or why not? How is this different from simply being "happy"?

4. Are you hungry for God? Do you want his best "food" for you? As you think about "spiritual menu items," what changes will you need to make in order to develop an intentional, healthy hunger for God?

5. You have been rescued from the murky waters of sin. Refer back to your list and pray that God will give you the courage to be a David to one person on your list.

Week Five - Read chapters eight and nine.
Scripture readings: Genesis 4:1-16; John 3:16; Ephesians 2:8-10; Colossians 1:15-20; Hebrews 1:3; 2:14-15

1. Spend some time thinking about these questions that Bruce asks: Is Jesus our Monarch or simply our mascot? Is Jesus our Creator or our convenience?

2. Think about "dress-up Christianity." Do you participate in it? If so, how? Have you ever been hurt by it?

3. What is the difference between appeasing God and pleasing God?

4. What limits have you placed on God in regard to serving him?

Week Six - Read chapters ten and eleven.
Scripture readings: Luke 9:57-62; 10:1-4; Colossians 4:12; James 1:19-25

1. Look at your list one last time. Have you made any sincere attempts to "be the aroma" to someone?

2. Excuses and wrong priorities make it difficult for us to give our life completely to God. How have you seen this reality to be true in life? Prayerfully consider the excuses you make concerning a deeper relationship with Christ.

3. Don't forget priorities. What are some things in your life that you need to prioritize so that you will not "hit the snooze button"?

4. As Bruce suggests, make a plan that will guide you into a deeper relationship with Christ and in turn will allow you to become the aroma you are called to be.

The Author

Bruce Hamsher is a pastor at Berlin (Ohio) Mennonite Church and a certified pastoral counselor and life coach. He holds a master's of ministry degree from the Masters International School of Divinity and a bachelor's in sociology from Mount Vernon Nazarene University. Bruce lives in Sugarcreek, Ohio, with his wife, Jocelyn, and their three sons.